FIRE ENGINES
UP CLOSE

★ **Andra Serlin Abramson** ★

STERLING

New York / London
www.sterlingpublishing.com/kids

Library of Congress Cataloging-in-Publication Data

Abramson, Andra Serlin.
 Fire engires up close / Andra Serlin Abramson.
     p. cm.
 Includes index.
 ISBN-13: 978-1-4027-4798-4
 ISBN-10: 1-4027-4798-5
 1. Fire engines--Juvenile literature. I. Title.

TH9372.A27 2008
628.9'259--dc22

                              2007008214

10 9 8 7 6 5 4 3 2 1

Published by Sterling Publishing Co., Inc.
387 Park Avenue South, New York, NY 10016
© 2007 by Sterling Publishing Co., Inc.
Distributed in Canada by Sterling Publishing
c/o Canadian Manda Group, 165 Dufferin Street
Toronto, Ontario, Canada M6K 3H6
Distributed in the United Kingdom by GMC Distribution Services
Castle Place, 166 High Street, Lewes, East Sussex, England BN7 1XU
Distributed in Australia by Capricorn Link (Australia) Pty. Ltd.
P.O. Box 704, Windsor, NSW 2756, Australia

Cover and interior design: Oxygen Design, Tilman Reitzle, Sherry Williams
Cover photo credits:
        Gilbert King: front cover (all photos except for front of engine); front flap (background and bottom); back flap (background);
                back cover (middle)
        © Robert Pernell / Shutterstock: front cover (front of engine)
        © Wernher Krutein / Photovault: back cover (top); front flap (middle)
        © Tobias Bernhard / zefa / CORBIS: front flap (top)
        © William Gottlieb / CORBIS: back flap (left)
        © Alan Schein Photography / CORBIS: back flap (right)
        © Thorsten Mischke / zefa / CORBIS: back cover (bottom)

Printed in Thailand

Sterling ISBN-13: 978-1-4027-4798-4
        ISBN-10: 1-4027-4798-5

For information about custom editions, special sales, premium
and corporate purchases, please contact Sterling Special Sales
Department at 800-805-5489 or specialsales@sterlingpub.com.

CONTENTS

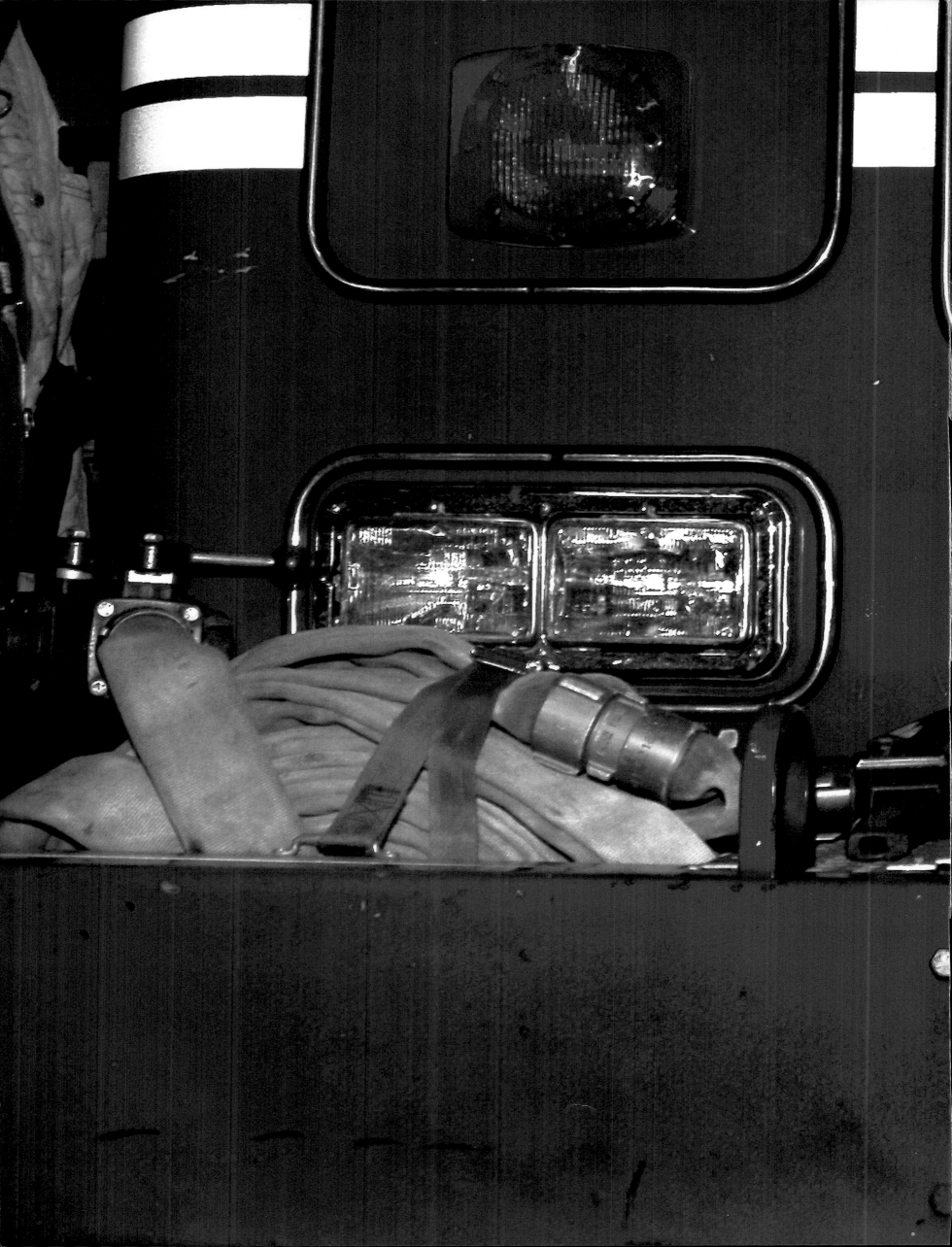

HERE COME THE TRUCKS!

YOU'VE SEEN THEM RACING TO THE SCENE of a fire or emergency, sirens screaming and horns blaring. They're fire engines, rescue vehicles we depend on to keep us safe and sound. From big ladder trucks to sleek pumper trucks, fire department vehicles carry the firefighters and equipment needed to put out fires and rescue both people from burning buildings and the occasional cat stuck in a tree.

Some fire engines are a greenish-yellow color, which is easier for our eyes to see in the dark.

Although we use the terms interchangeably, a fire truck is actually different from a fire engine. Fire engines carry their own water supply, while fire trucks carry additional firefighting equipment and other emergency gear, such as rescue tools, ladders, and extrication equipment.

Back when horses were used to pull fire equipment, Dalmations kept them company during the long waits between fires, guarding the horses and keeping them from wandering off.

IN THE HOUSE

THE FIREHOUSE IS THE HEART of the fire company. It provides overnight accommodations for firefighters on duty and comes complete with a kitchen, common rooms, and plenty of companionship.

When firefighters are not fighting a fire, they still have plenty to do at the firehouse. The crew takes turns doing the housework and cooking the meals. They also maintain their gear. From washing the fire engines to hanging the hoses to dry, they make sure that all of the equipment is ready for the next emergency.

Firefighters take turns doing the cooking and cleaning at the firehouse.

Look Out Below!

When not on call, firefighters usually spend their time on the upper levels of the firehouse where the living quarters, kitchen, and common areas can be found. The fire pole allows firefighters to get from the upper level down to the first floor—where the fire engines are located— as quickly as possible.

Firefighters always park the fire engine facing out so that they can pull out quickly on the way to a fire.

The first fire pole was installed in the house of Chicago's Engine Company No. 21 in 1878. The company was almost always the first to arrive on the scene of a fire, so eventually fire poles were installed in every firehouse in Chicago.

BECOMING A FIREFIGHTER

FIREFIGHTING CAN BE a very dangerous job. The brave men and women who risk their lives to save others know that any mistakes they make might kill or injure themselves or someone else. In the United States, the National Fire Academy is located in Emmitsburg, Maryland, and is where firefighters and other emergency workers are trained to deal more effectively with fire and related emergencies.

A student will train for 600 hours over the course of 14 weeks to become a firefighter. After leaving school, firefighters spend one year learning on the job before they can graduate. They are called "probies" because they are "on probation" until they have proven themselves over the course of the year.

Training to be a firefighter can be stressful and exhausting. Firefighters must be able to handle many different types of emergencies.

PUMPER TRUCKS

PUMPER TRUCKS CARRY THE HOSES needed to fight fires and are usually the first fire engines to arrive at a fire. It is their job to get the hoses hooked up to a water source, such as a fire hydrant. Then they spray water on the building to get it cooled down enough so that firefighters can enter it. The amount and force of the water are both controlled by a pump panel. Firefighters who work on pumper trucks are sometimes called "smoke eaters" because they breathe in (or "eat up") so much smoke.

Pumper trucks can carry many feet of hose, but sometimes more hose is needed. Some fire departments have special hose trucks that carry hundreds of feet of extra hose for pumper trucks to use.

And More Pumper Trucks . . .

A rescue pumper carries specialized rescue equipment in addition to a water tank that can hold up to 500 gallons of water. Rescue pumper trucks generally carry fewer feet of hose compared to traditional pumper trucks. A super pumper truck has a water cannon that can shoot water up to 500 feet into the air. That's enough for it to go over another building and hit a target a block away!

Gauges help firefighters monitor the pressure of the water pumping through the hose. PSI stands for pounds per square inch.

What it Takes

Being a firefighter is a difficult job, and becoming a firefighter is difficult, too. Before men and women can even begin training, they must pass a physical test. A firefighter may need to carry an injured person down several flights of stairs, or he or she may need to help carry a heavy hose close to a fire. Both of these acts require a lot of strength. After prospective firefighters show that they can handle the physical aspects of the job, they start their training, learning everything from the proper way to fold a hose to the best way to climb a ladder.

One of the most well-known fires in history is the Great Chicago Fire of 1871. Legend has it that the fire started when a cow kicked over a kerosene lantern in a barn. While this story has been proven to be false, more than one-third of the city was destroyed in the fire.

These volunteer firefighters in Rockville, Maryland, are prepared for when the alarm sounds.

Even when a fire is out, there is still work for firefighters to do at the scene.

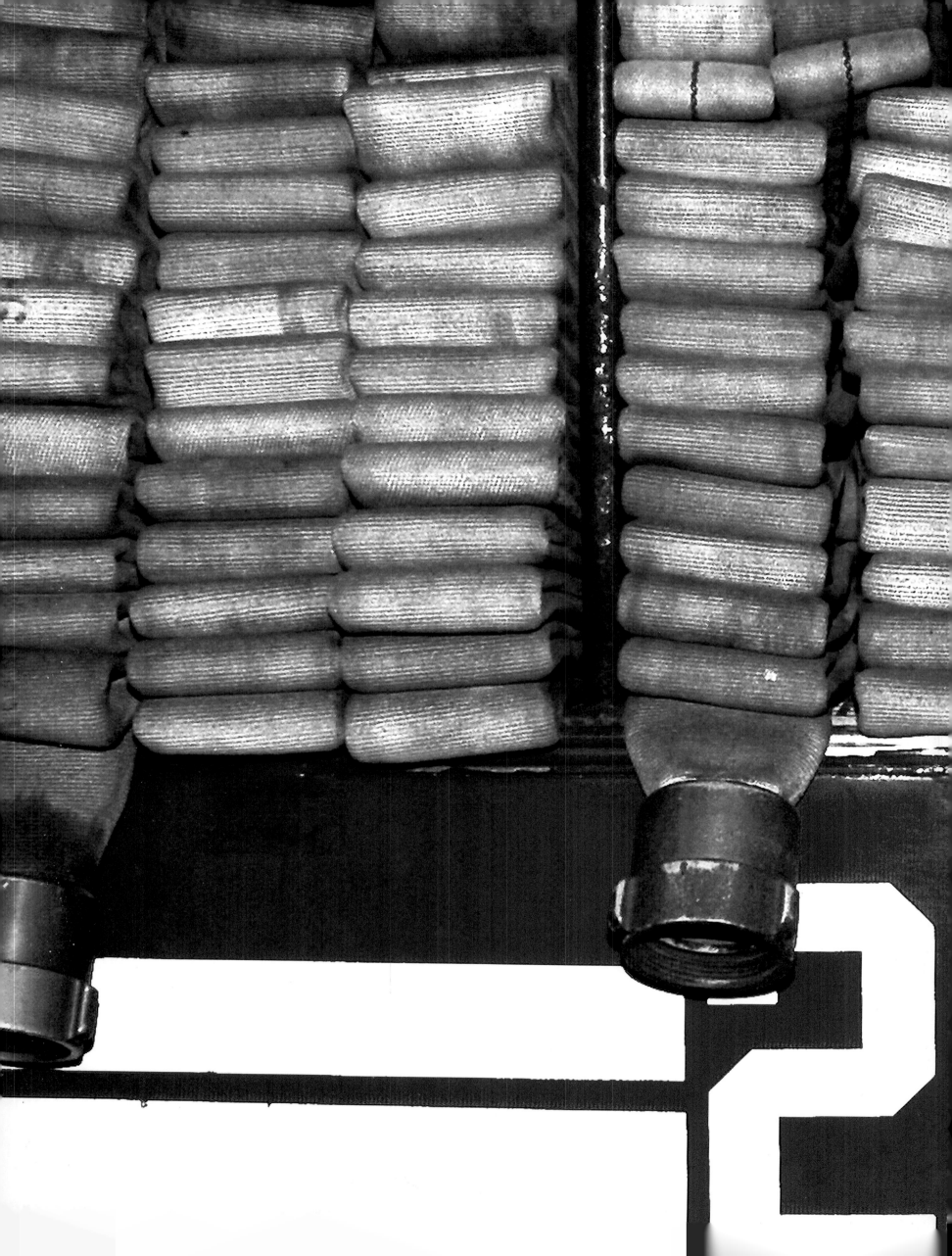

How to handle a hose is just one skill firefighters need to master.

LAYING IN

WHEN HOSES ARE HOOKED UP TO A PUMPER truck or a fire hydrant and the water starts pumping, that's when the hard work really begins. Firefighters may have to carry the heavy hoses up stairs or ladders to bring the hoses as close to the fire as they can. It can take three or more firefighters to handle one hose because a hose full of water can be as heavy as a steel pipe. The hose may be so stiff that it cannot go around corners. When firefighters bring a hose close to a fire, they say they are "laying in" or "stretching in" the hose.

When they are not being used, hoses are folded or rolled up for easy access. Some fire trucks can carry hundreds or even thousands of feet of hose.

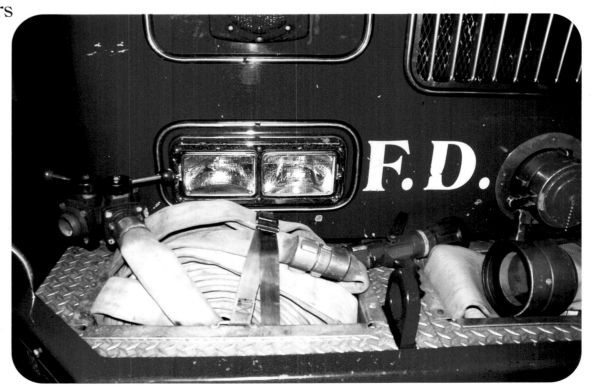

Way Back When

Before hoses were invented, people put out a fire by throwing buckets of water on it. In larger towns, neighbors would form "bucket brigades," in which lines of people stood in line and passed full and empty buckets up and down between a fire and a source of water, such as a stream or a well. Not surprisingly, a lot of buildings (and even whole towns) burned to the ground with this inefficient system of firefighting.

A fire hydrant is sometimes called a "fireplug." This is because firefighters used to make holes in the public water pipes to fight fires. After the fire was out, the holes would be plugged with stoppers. These stoppers became known as fireplugs. Fireplugs date back to at least the 1600s.

In this photo from World War II, German civilians form a bucket brigade in an attempt to quench a fire in their village.

After a fire is out, firefighters use teamwork to put back all of their equipment. One of the biggest jobs is folding up the fire hose.

Working together under dangerous conditions means that firefighters must learn to depend on each other.

MEET YOUR FIRE COMPANY

A FIRE COMPANY CONSISTS OF an officer, such as a captain or lieutenant, and several firefighters. Each company specializes in a certain task. For example, large cities may have both rescue companies—ladder or "truck" companies—and engine companies on hand to respond to different emergencies.

Fire companies often follow a "two in, two out" rule, which says that two firefighters must always enter and leave a building together. This buddy system makes sure that no one gets lost or left behind during the chaotic conditions of a fire.

Talk Like a Firefighter

Firefighters have their own words and phrases that describe what they do. Some words describe different types of fires. For example, if a firefighter says a fire is "ripe," it means that it is hot and smoky. If a fire is "a worker," it means that the firefighters will have to work very hard to put it out.

Some words firefighters use relate to what they do to put out a fire. A "fire line" (or a "fire break") is a strip of land that firefighters clear to keep forest fires from spreading. Firefighters might say they have "ventilated" a building. This means that they have opened the windows and doors, and chopped holes in the roof to let the smoke and heat out of the building.

Cutting a hole in the roof of a burning building allows smoke and heat to escape. This makes it safer for firefighters to enter the building.

When at the firehouse, firefighters take care of the engines and other equipment, but they still have time for a bit of fun.

NO. 2
SCHARGE

NO. 3
2 1/2"

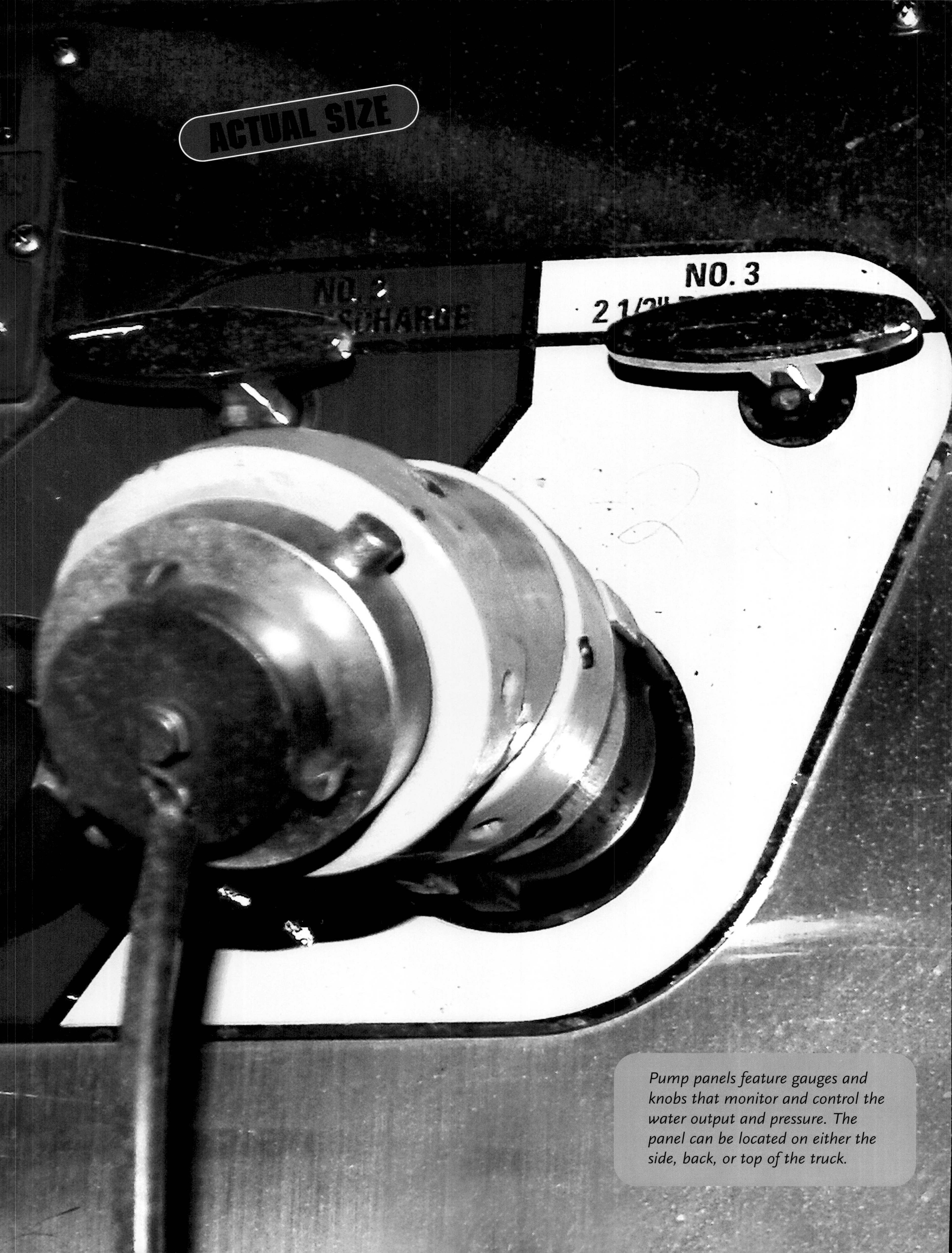

Pump panels feature gauges and knobs that monitor and control the water output and pressure. The panel can be located on either the side, back, or top of the truck.

A ladder truck is so long that it often has two drivers. The driver in the back is called a "tillerman." The tillerman's job is to steer the rear wheels of the ladder truck.

ACTUAL SIZE

RING THE BELL

IF YOU LIVE NEAR A FIREHOUSE, you may have heard the fire alarm that alerts firefighters of a fire nearby. Sometimes there may be one call of the bell. Sometimes there may be as many as five. The size of a fire is indicated by the number of bells sounded. A one-alarm fire is small and requires just one fire company to respond. A five-alarm fire is big, needing the help of multiple fire companies.

SOUND THE SIRENS

IN ORDER TO GET TO A FIRE or emergency as quickly as possible, fire engines are equipped with sirens and lights that warn people to make way and watch out for the speeding trucks. The controls for the lights and sirens are located on panels near the driver of the truck. New technology allows fire trucks to control the traffic light system, changing the lights to green as they approach, so that they can avoid accidents that are sometimes caused by fire trucks running through red lights.

The cab of a fire truck needs to be well laid-out so firefighters can see where everything is.

Sometimes the ladder on a fire truck is the only way to get to people trapped inside a building.

LADDER TRUCKS

. . . .

FIGHTING FIRES IN TALL BUILDINGS requires a ladder truck. Firefighters extend the ladder of the truck to get onto the high floors of high-rise buildings. They allow people trapped on the higher floors to get to the ground. The longest ladder on a fire truck is called an "aerial ladder," which can extend up to 10 floors.

Ladders on a ladder truck are as long as the truck itself—often longer!

Under Control

The control panel for an aerial ladder is located on the back of the ladder truck. The ladders are attached to turntables that allow them to turn 360 degrees. The ladder controls require just one firefighter to change the position and length of the ladder. It can take as many as six firefighters to raise a 40-foot ladder by hand, so this is a vast improvement.

Firefighters who work for a Ladder Truck Company are responsible for search and rescue, forcible entry, ventilation of a structure during a fire, and the use of ladders to rescue people above ground level.

Some ladders have a bucket at the top that provides a safe place for the firefighter to stand while the ladder is moving.

TOP

○ ○ ○ 10' PIKE WOOD

○ ○ ○ 10' PIKE WOOD

○ 10' HALLIGAN W/GAS

○ ○ 10' HALL. W/GAS

○ ○ 8' ROCK

○ ○ 8' ROCK

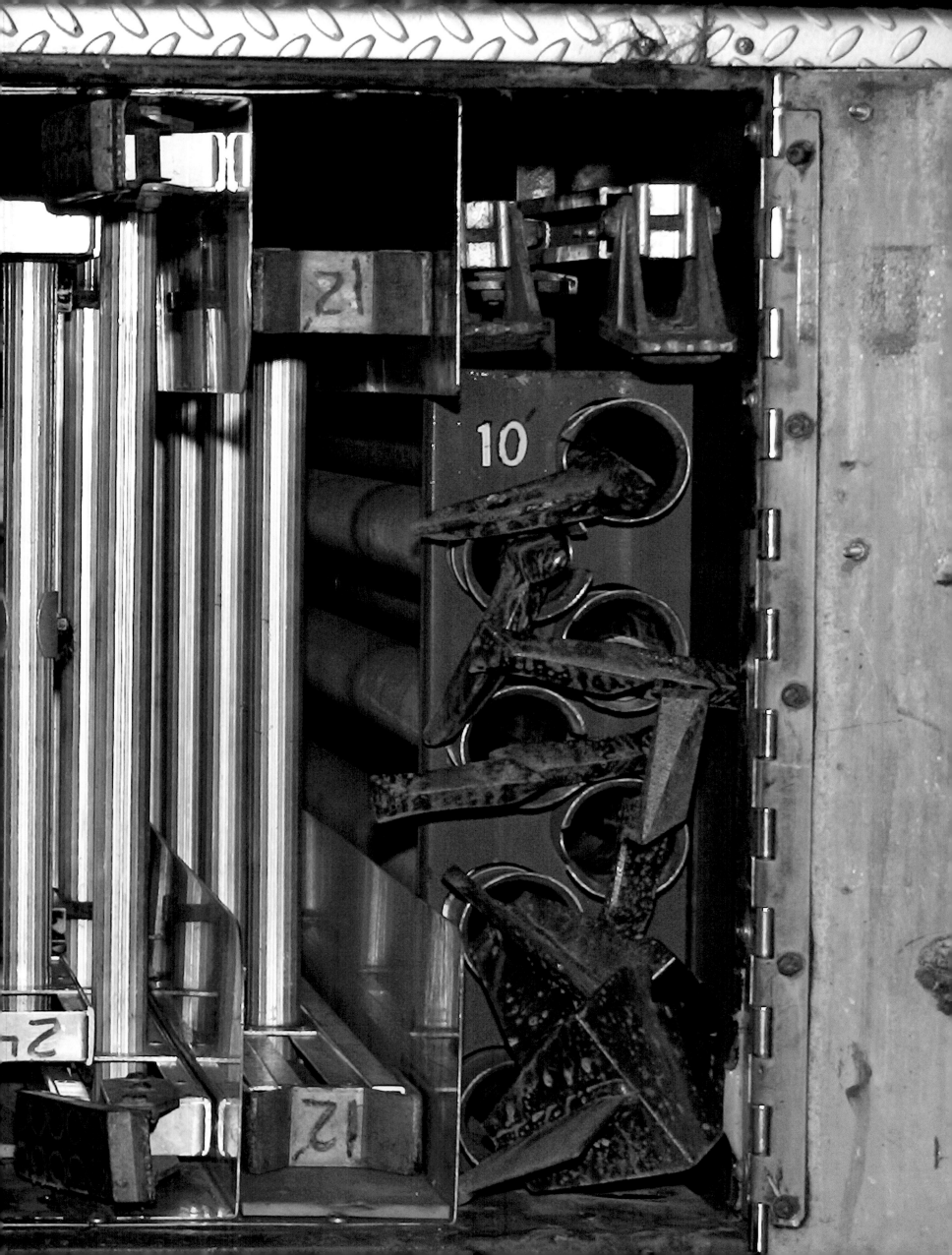

SAFETY GEAR

FIREFIGHTERS WEAR big, metal helmets that are designed to protect a firefighter's head from both flames and falling debris. During a fire, there is always the danger of a roof caving in or other material falling down. Without proper headgear, firefighters would be risking their lives even more than they already are.

Firefighters also wear special pants, coats, and boots that are designed to keep them safe. The outfits are called "turnouts" because they are worn when firefighters "turn out" (or "show up") when there is a fire or other emergency.

Firefighters keep their suits and helmets hung up and ready to go so that they can get dressed quickly.

Fire helmets need to fit well in order to provide effective protection against flames and falling objects. Most helmets have an adjustable headband and chinstrap.

These firefighters could not enter this burning building without SCBAs.

Self-Contained Breathing Apparatus

A Self-Contained Breathing Apparatus, also known as an SCBA, helps firefighters breathe clean air while fighting smoky fires. An SCBA has three parts. The first part is a high-pressure tank carrying compressed oxygen. This is connected to a regulator that controls the flow of air. The regulator is connected to a mouthpiece or mask that goes over the firefighter's face. All three parts are also attached to a harness strapped on the firefighter's back so that both hands can remain free. SCBAs are sometimes referred to as "airpacks."

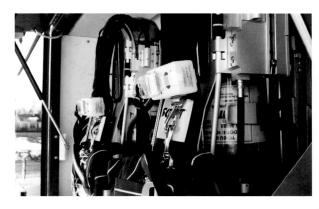

SCBAs are stored at the ready in fire trucks.

Some firefighting suits are coated with metal. The metal reflects heat, keeping the firefighter from getting burned. However, the metal is heavy, which can make it difficult for firefighters to move around.

This firefighter is ready to enter a burning building.

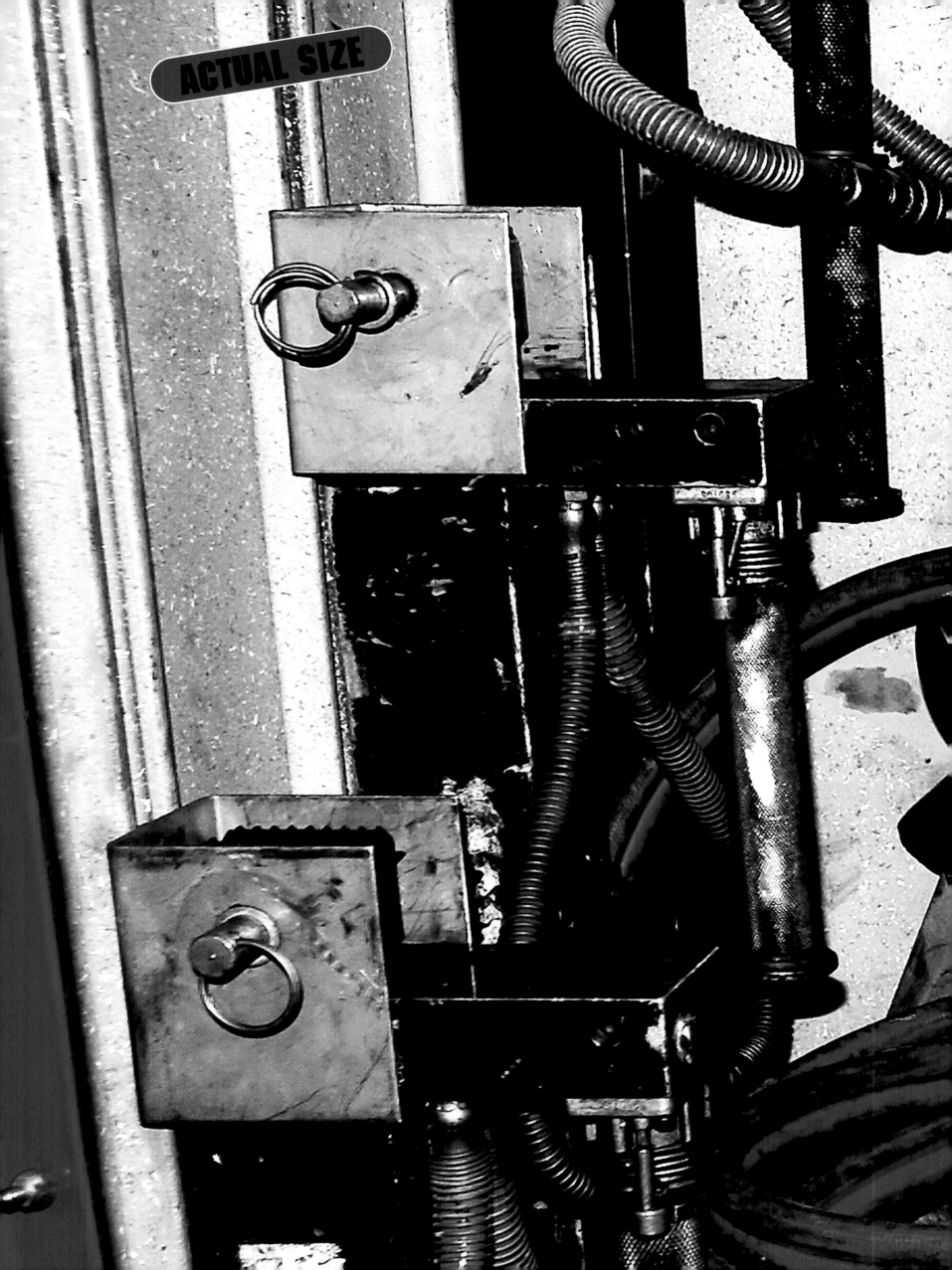

ACTUAL SIZE

FIREFIGHTING AND RESCUE EQUIPMENT

IN ADDITION TO HOSES AND LADDERS, firefighters use a variety of other equipment to save lives and extinguish fires. Some ladder trucks are called "hook and ladder trucks" because they carry hooks and other tools that can be used to tear down walls and cut through floors to get to the fire. Firefighters who use hooks are called "hookies."

A landing net is carried on the side of the fire truck, but it is used only as a last resort when a trapped person cannot or will not wait for a ladder. A landing net is only safe when used below the fourth floor of a building.

Hooks are often taller than firefighters!

High-powered nozzles help firefighters put out fires quickly.

The Jaws of Life are used to pry open vehicles as quickly as possible to get to people trapped inside. There are three parts to the Jaws of Life: cutters, spreaders, and rams.

Axes, wrenches, saws, and the Jaws of Life are just some examples of the equipment used by firefighters.

This portable spotlight enables firefighters to investigate the scene after a fire has been extinguished.

There are many different kinds of nozzles that can be attached to hoses—all are stored in a special compartment on the truck.

This rescue equipment has been used to save lives in hundreds of emergencies.

THE DELUGE PUMP

THE DELUGE PUMP, ALSO KNOWN AS THE DELUGE GUN, is a special nozzle used by firefighters to spray up to 2,000 gallons of water per minute on a fire. Deluge guns are often mounted on the top of fire engines. They may also have more than one nozzle so that water can be sprayed in different directions at the same time. There is even a freestanding deluge pump that can be placed near the fire and left alone, freeing up firefighters to take on other tasks.

Deluge pumps can spray water hundreds of feet into the air.

Firefighters use fog to keep a fire contained and prevent it from spreading. Fog droplets are so small that they can stop fires without damaging clothing, furniture, artwork, and other belongings.

Beyond Water

Water doesn't work with putting out gasoline fires because the gas is able to float on top of the water and stay ignited. Gasoline fires can be put out with a foam that is made by adding chemicals to water to produce a mass of bubbles. The foam prevents air from getting to the flames. Fire needs air to keep burning, so the foam stops the fire by smothering it.

To keep a fire from spreading, this firefighter has sprayed foam on the entire area.

Deluge pumps help firefighters get the maximum amount of water where it needs to go.

FIREFIGHTING AROUND THE WORLD

THE VERY FIRST FIRE ENGINES were developed in England in the 1700s. These first engines were pulled by people, and it took 20 or more strong men to pull an engine. Once the engine reached the fire, it then had to be pumped by hand. It could take a dozen men to pump enough water to put out even a small fire. Today, fire engines in England, Canada, and across the world have the high-tech equipment designed to put a fire out as quickly as possible.

This fire engine—assigned to the Halifax, Nova Scotia, airport—is on hand in case of an accident.

French firefighters are called *sapeurs-pompiers*. They handle more than 3.6 million emergencies a year, ranging from fires to car accidents to stuck elevators.

Firefighters are extinguishing a fire after the collision of a train and a truck in northern France.

UN TRAIN PEUT EN CACHER UN AUTRE

International Crews

Firefighter units in England are called "brigades." Brigades are then divided into stations that each have at least one pumper engine. The average size of a crew for a British station is five. Some countries, such as Finland, operate their fire crews with four to six firefighters. The engine carries the unit leader, an engineer, and two to four firefighters, depending on the size and intensity of the fire.

We all know that the number to call in case of emergency in the United States is 9-1-1. However, in Germany the number to call is 1-1-2. Although firefighters around the world may name things differently, most use the same type of equipment and technology to fight fires.

On November 20, 1992, Windsor Castle near London, England, caught fire. It took nearly 40 fire engines and more than 200 firefighters to put out the blaze. Luckily, no one was seriously injured in the fire.

Rescue vehicles line the streets near a train station in Bologna, Italy. In countries around the world, firefighters and other rescue personnel are always at the ready to help in whatever way they can.

Index

Photo Credits